To The Wilder Family

From Becky & girl O'Reilly

Flavia

Welcome To The World
copyright © 1993 by Flavia Weedn
All rights reserved. Printed in Hong Kong.

For information write Andrews and McMeel,
a Universal Press Syndicate Company,
4900 Main Street, Kansas City, Missouri 64112

ISBN: 0-8362-4704-3

WELCOME
TO THE WORLD

Written and Illustrated
by Flavia Weedn

It

is the

morning

of your life

sweet

baby...

and all

of your

dreams

are

just

beginning.

Your

heart

is filled

with wonder

for you

are made of

lullabies and love.

FLAVIA

You

have

no way

of knowing

but

you hold

all of our

tomorrows

tenderly

in your

hands.

FLAVIA

You are a warm

and wondrous

gift to the heart.

Welcome

to the

world

dear

little

one.

May

God

bless

you

forever

and

ever.

Flavia at work in her Santa Barbara studio

Flavia Weedn is a writer, painter and philosopher. Her life's work is about hope for the human spirit. "I want to reach people of all ages who have never been told, 'wait a minute, look around you. It's wonderful to be alive and every one of us matters. We can make a difference if we keep trying and never give up.'" It is Flavia's and her family's wish to awaken this spirit in each and every one of us. Flavia's messages are translated into many foreign languages on giftware, books and paper goods around the world.

To find out more about Flavia write to:
Weedn Studios, Ltd.
740 State Street, 3rd Floor
Santa Barbara, CA 93101 USA
or call: 805-564-6909